LIFE WITH MY
HORSES

JEAN MCFADDIN

BALBOA.PRESS

A DIVISION OF HAY HOUSE

Balboa Press books may be ordered through booksellers or by contacting:

Balboa Press
A Division of Hay House
1663 Liberty Drive
Bloomington, IN 47403
www.balboapress.com
844-682-1282

Because of the dynamic nature of the Internet, any web addresses or
links contained in this book may have changed since publication and
may no longer be valid. The views expressed in this work are solely those
of the author and do not necessarily reflect the views of the publisher,
and the publisher hereby disclaims any responsibility for them.

The author of this book does not dispense medical advice or prescribe the use
of any technique as a form of treatment for physical, emotional, or medical
problems without the advice of a physician, either directly or indirectly. The
intent of the author is only to offer information of a general nature to help
you in your quest for emotional and spiritual well-being. In the event you use
any of the information in this book for yourself, which is your constitutional
right, the author and the publisher assume no responsibility for your actions.

Any people depicted in stock imagery provided by Getty Images are
models, and such images are being used for illustrative purposes only.
Certain stock imagery © Getty Images.

Print information available on the last page.

ISBN: 978-1-9822-6123-8 (sc)
ISBN: 978-1-9822-6125-2 (hc)
ISBN: 978-1-9822-6124-5 (e)

Balboa Press rev. date: 01/22/2021

CONTENTS

INTRODUCTION

When you read this small collection of horse stories, be sure that you understand that these are my personal experiences. I am not a veterinarian nor a professional trainer, even though I have countless hours working closely with both.

Everyone has their own idea of how things should be done and that is fine. There is always room for learning and I hope that my experiences give you a different perspective of what can and will happen if you are a horse owner.

We must always keep an open mind to the fact that there are more than one way to do things.

These stories reflect my knowledge and my approach to hands on horsemanship, my way.

FOREWORD

I have thought for a very long time about sharing my experiences in equine ownership. So this book is a small collection of stories about my love and life with our large pet, the horse.

Loving horses and wishing for one began at a very young age. You will read where my earlier experiences occurred at my grandmother's home in Louisiana.

Quite some time later, as a young mother, I would take my two children almost every summer to a dude ranch where we all enjoyed riding in groups and participating in games. Of course the horses would already be tacked up so all we had to do was get on the horse. No one ever took the time or had the time to explain putting on the saddle or bridle.

So in that respect we did not learn "tacking up" or the function of bit/bridle. Just hold on and follow the leader. Sure was fun.

A few years later I decided to purchase two horses. Cost was not that much, but for a working mother of two it was really something I had no business purchasing. As it was, I was living paycheck to paycheck. Along with these two horses, the gentleman convinced me to purchase a third horse, boney Molly. You will read about her later in a story.

So now we are owners of the two "riding horses" and Molly. We bought a used saddle, bridle and bit and put them on the horse the way we thought it should go. Only by the grace of God did we not get hurt.

The mare was just one of those horses that would put up with anything.

We found out very soon that the gelding did not know what whoa meant and no bit of any kind would help you stop or control him. He was sold.

Much time passed. At the age of thirty four, after Gus and I had been married a while we purchased our first Arabian mare. This started our journey into Arabian horse breeding. Then later on as breeders of the straight Egyptian Arabian.

In the beginning I knew nothing about horses except where they ate, where they pooped and that I loved them.

With the help and patience of Dr. Sherwood, our friend and veterinarian for 45 or so years, I slowly began learning how to care for horses, ie feeding, immunizations, deworming, breeding and foaling.

When I say slowly, I mean slowly. Almost everyday something would come up and I needed to call Dr. Sherwood. Hereinafter I will refer to Dr. Sherwood as Dr. S. He probably could write a comical book with all the dumb questions I asked. I learned so much from him.

Gus and I began attending many clinics and seminars. We would be sitting and listening and it seemed as though we had heard the same information over and over. But maybe we didn't know at the time but one little thing would be put in the back of our mind that just might come in handy someday. Yep

You must keep in mind that you will never know everything. Just when you thought you had experienced it all, you have not. There is always something new happening right around the corner. I tell horse enthusiasts that all the time. Keep an open mind. Keep learning.

I have always felt there was a need to teach potential horse owners what I personally have learned about horses.

For several years I had equine summer camps here at the ranch for both juniors and adult. The name of the camp was CAMP IWANNAOWNA. I have been asked "did you teach then to ride"?

I would say yes, but that is the least thing I taught them. We taught them how to halter and lead a horse and how to be safe around them. How to keep the horse from stepping on them. They learned proper grooming and hoof care as well.

We taught them anatomy so they would understand the function of the horse; how and what he sees and how he moves. Immunizations, deworming programs and nutrition were important. Feed and hay, yes but most important is for there to be adequate water for horses at all times.

We explained definition of tack and how it is correctly applied for the function of the horse. And no, tack is not something you find at a hardware store.

Then and only then were we ready to ride. Oh yes, don't forget your helmet. We can fix broken arms, but the head...?

One last recommendation I have always had for potential horse buyers.

DON'T BE IN A HURRY. There are a lot of horse dealers out there. So buyer BEWARE.

If you get anything out of my experiences I will feel that this writing was worth it.

This is not my quote, but my favorite.

"THERE IS SOMETHING ABOUT THE OUTSIDE OF A HORSE THAT IS GOOD FOR THE INSIDE OF A MAN"

PLUM NEARLY RANCH

GUS AND JEAN MCFADDIN-How It All Began

The first thing a person asks when hearing the name of the ranch is "where did that name originate". The name actually came from one of our employees, when she was asked where she worked, her reply was "Plum Nelly" plum out of Beaumont and nelly (nearly) to Port Arthur. I will tell you right here and now, people remembered the ranch name when they couldn't remember our name.

Although we continued to search for a more classic name for the ranch, we always came back to PLUM NEARLY RANCH. Maybe it is corny but it is remembered. Yes, Plum Nearly Ranch is still in the same location. I wish I could say continuing to do the same things we did in the past, but since we have gotten older (can you imagine) and many of our horses that we still have are older too, we decided to cut way back and continue loving and caring for the ones we have.

This year (2020) we do have a foal due in May. We do not have many young horses here on the ranch. We have two that are 30 years old.

I am Jean McFaddin, often referred to as Miss Jean, the horse lady. I was a city girl turned country woman when I married my husband of 52 years. G.A.N. McFaddin that everyone knows as Gus.

When I was growing up, my mother was very protective of me and my sister Patsy. Mother didn't want her girls to get dirty or participate in any activity where we might get hurt. I, for instance, was still riding a tricycle when all my friends were on bicycles. Mother thought the tricycle was safer. So here I would go peddling BEHIND all my friends.

The only horse experience I had, as a child was when I visited my grandparents in Louisiana. That's when I met the little horse named Fanny. In my young adult life I owned horses, when really I shouldn't have. Purchasing a horse is the least expense of owning a horse and that soon became apparent. When I bought my first horse, I only knew three things...where they ate, where they pooped and that I loved them. Looking back, I know the good Lord had to be watching over me. You have heard the expression that you were riding by the seat of your pants? Well that was me. I really didn't know what made a horse "tick" or the function of the tack used on the horse. I just played it by ear and that was not a good idea.

One must realize that the horse is a very large animal that has a mind of it's own. You may be going in one direction when all of a sudden the horse decides to go the other. At this point you are probably on the ground. You are not in control...you just think you are.

I have been a hands on horse owner riding and showing our horses for many years. I have never grown out of the love for the horses. I still want them around. If the going gets tough for you just put a grooming brush in your hand and spend some time with your horse. This is a great way to bond with your horse and clear your mind.

Here is how my journey evolved. Gus and I married in 1968.

We have resided at our original location on West Port Arthur Rd since that time. When we first married, we had a small amount of acreage with an old shed row barn out back that we never used. We never talked about owning horses.

After about five years, out of the clear blue, Gus decided to buy an Arabian filly from our very dear friend, Dr. George Campbell. George had just casually mentioned that his mare had just foaled a filly.

Gus had been introduced to the Arabian horse when he was a student at Culver Academy. He said the Arabian horse is like having a big dog for a pet. They love people. For thousand and thousand of years the Arabian horse lived inside the tents with their Bedouin owners. Some probably do even today. The horse was very important to their survival. The Arabian horse took them to fight their enemies and to gather their food.

That is the reason it is inbred in the Arabian Horse to be a 'people horse'.

One Arabian filly...well that started it all. From that day the number of horses at Plum Nearly Ranch began to grow. We traveled to Arabian farms and auctions all over the country and got into the Arabian horse breeding program big time. Over a period of time our interest gradually focused toward just breeding the Egyptian Arabian horse. By then I was in "hog heaven". Whoops, I mean horse heaven.

We attended and participated in many clinics and seminars regarding horse care, horse management, breeding and foaling. With that and more came lessons learned from trial and error, trial and error, trial and error.

We have learned hands on is by far the best and only way to be a horse owner. The most important mentor for me has been our veterinarian of 45 years, Dr. Sherwood.

Second to hands-on and perhaps as a result of hands-on one must think like a horse.

When I was young I loved riding horses and if there had been someone nearby to teach me the basics of horsemanship, I would have been first in line.

For that reason I began having equine summer camps for both juniors and adults. I named the camp Iwannaowna. As in many people want to own horses and don't know anything about them. (Just like me earlier) I thought if I could pass on the information I had learned over the years as I said with trial and error and keeping an open mind, maybe it would keep someone from being injured and hopefully make their transition to horse ownership a bit easier.

The most important part of the camp was teaching safety on and around horses. We instructed anatomy, grooming, parasite control, feed programs, tack and tack adjustments.

Lessons started with the nose and worked towards the tail. Total care was the objective. After that....we taught them horseback riding.

I loved these summer camps and I still have contact with many of the juniors and adults that had participated. The juniors are all grown up but many still stay in touch with me. It has been great to have this connection with so many people.

Many times the camps opened the door for people interested in obtaining their first horse and getting into the horsemanship world, big time. Some thank me, others say, why didn't you warn me? Like most things we purchase and love, one is not enough. Horses, that is.

In 1996 George W. Bush, then Governor, appointed me to

the Texas State Board of Veterinary Medical Examiners. I was one of three lay people that served along with three veterinarians. This was a six year appointment and a real eye opener. The board not only licensed veterinarians but heard many cases supposedly mal practice ones on the part of the veterinarian. Rarely did we suspend or withdraw any veterinarian's license. Occasionally there was a reprimand and/or fines. The cases were always interesting. Many if not most of the complaints were of a frivolous nature and were not acted upon. It was indeed a great honor to serve on this board for the State of Texas.

In years past at Plum Nearly Ranch we would have approximately ten foals born each year and I would be in attendance to almost all births. Each time that big/little foal enters into the world, it is truly a miracle.

Even though it is said that horses in the wild seem to do just fine without any help when they are foaling, I thought otherwise. They really needed me, or was it I really needed them?

I have kept a foaling diary for these foaling events and it is really interesting to see that they, mare and foal, are all different. You think you know when, where and how, but you really don't.

The old saying 'don't mess with Mother Nature' somehow doesn't apply during foaling season.

As Gus and I have gotten older, our herd of Arabian horses has been reduced quite a bit. We may have a foal every now and then. We have very few young ones left to breed. We do however have many senior citizens. Two geldings that are 30 at this time. Going strong.

Five years ago a foal began her entrance into this world at 10 PM. Oh great I thought. Foal born, things done, back to bed.

Well that just didn't happen. There were no major problems but this was a new game for this mare. She was a maiden mare and nineteen years old. Her teats were not full and in fact they were very small and it appeared she was not producing enough of the milk/colostrum. I did have the medication (Oxytocin) that I could give by injection to help with this problem. (Prior instructions from Dr. S.) I administered the injection and waited.

After a while it seemed to be working. Picture this if you can. Me kneeling down, milking the mare (to get milk on my fingers) while balancing foal in nursing position with my body, twitching the mare's shoulder with my other hand so that she would be more cooperative. Very gently, that is. While I am under the mare getting milk on my fingers I am also guiding foal's head toward the udder. Milk on fingers, smell of milk, surely the foal would catch on. Well that did not happen at that time.

You must know that you cannot force them at this point. You can lead them to water/milk but you can't make them drink.

So I would try this procedure and if not successful, I would let the mare and foal rest. (and me). Fifteen to twenty minutes later I would try again. In between the several times that I had tried getting the foal to nurse, I would sit outside the stall door just biding my time. By now it is well past midnight. I had been in and out of the stall so many times that when I was sitting in the hallway, I would sometime cough. When I did, the filly would whinny at me as if to say " hey out there, let's get this action going".

About the fourth time we were a bit successful. The foal was in the right position, really hungry now and searching for the faucets. Then she latched on, but not for long.

At this time I am barely twitching the mare and guiding the foal with my body. In this awkward position I am thinking, am I getting too old for this? All the while in this position, I am softly talking to the mare and assuring her it was ok. We were doing good.

Still I could not go in the house to bed. I had to wait to

make sure the foal would continue nursing and the mare would cooperate. We all know how important the colostrum is to the foal.

Every now and then I would hear the mare squeal a little so I would go back into the stall and just hold her lightly and talk to her ever so softly. Easy girl, good girl.

You don't want this process to be marred by negative input so your soothing voice is important. This is all happening between midnight and three in the morning.

Still not sure that all is going well. Time passed slowly and each time I would hear the slight squeal I would repeat the process. They were now doing great.

It is now 5:30 a.m. Mother you should see me now. I am a mess. I have amniotic fluid, urine and colostrum all over me.

Before going inside I leave a note for my employee stating the time of departure (me) asking her to give the mare another injection of the Oxytocin and to make sure foal is continuing to nurse. And oh yes, please take all calls and let me sleep.

It is 5:30 a.m. The stars are out, birds chirping, chickens crowing and dogs barking off in a distance and I am strolling toward the house for a shower and a warm bed.

Am I tired? A little. Am I too old? Maybe. But I can say the experience of the night has me rejuvenated. It is so worth all the tiring work and sleepless night. Another miracle and I was part of it.

To me, this was a new year. The birth of a foal starts a horse owner's New Year.

That's how it all began. The following stories are my experiences, lessons learned. Laughter and tears told through some of the horses I have known and loved.

I would imagine that many other stories could be told by friends and family that worked right beside me. They have been right there with me to experience the good times and the bad. Being excited when a new foal is born and consoling me when a beloved horse had to be put down.

That's life…that's horse owner life.

FANNIE

Was Her Name....

You can say...it was all Fannie's fault....fault that I learned early in life that I loved horses...all four legged horses...white...brown... black..didn't matter just loved horses.

My only exposure to horses up close that is, was when we traveled to my grandparents farm in Louisiana when I was just five or six years old.

There Fannie was...short, fat and beautiful. But aren't they all beautiful? I would beg my uncle to let me ride and sure enough he would tack her up and let me get on. Now mind you I knew absolutely nothing, I mean nothing about riding a horse. My plan was to just sit there and hope that Fannie knew what to do and that she would not do anything foolish. I am amazed that my mother even let me within miles of that horse since she was so protective of me. Not only protective but surely didn't want me to get dirty in any way. Little Miss Clean, I was, but boy did I make up for it years later.

Anyway back to the Fannie era. Every time we visited my relatives in Louisiana the only thing I cared about doing was riding Fannie.

I soon began to pester my Uncle about when I could take Fannie home. Each time his answer was a put off, only I didn't see it that way. He would tell me that the next time I came he would make necessary arrangements for her to be taken back to Texas for me. Next visit there he would say we needed special papers to transport her. Next visit there was always an excuse as to why Fannie could not be taken at that time.

It took me a very long time before I finally realized that these excuses were my Uncle's way of softening a just plain NO. It was like a carrot in front of the donkey's nose. It just kept me going and going and going. Hoping, hoping and hoping.

Miraculously I had only one bad experience with Fannie. One day I was riding her, just walking around very slowly, minding my own business when one of my cousins jumped out from behind a bush, scared Fannie and off we went. Fannie ran under a clothes line. I stayed on but the clothesline scraped my neck just a bit. Nothing serious and in no way did it discourage me from wanting to be on Fannie every chance I got.

Fannie lived quite a while. Many years later, when I asked about her, my Uncle told me she had accidently been shot by a hunter.

How sad. Fannie was a good ole girl and she instilled in me the love that I still have for horses......all horses.

CHILDHOOD DREAM

To a Reality

A Childhood dream coming true at grandmotherhood, is the expression I have used many times, especially when I begin any of my horse tales.

I mentioned how protective my mother had been and o.k., maybe I didn't have as much freedom most children I knew, but my upbringing did not effect me, my entire life. On the contrary, I have spent most of my adult life making up for lost time.

I hope in sharing some of my horse experiences it will help you understand that in order to be a successful horse person, I repeat, you must think like a horse. This does not come easily but if you are truly a dedicated horse person you will come to understand this.

Understanding a Horse's Behavior... Why did my horse react that way? Was he frightened and nervous? If we made a change in his environment was that the reason?

New Experience...If I start to teach a young horse or an older one to load in the horse trailer, I think of how and what does he feel. Is it fear, or anxiety? What if I put a stable buddy in the trailer first that had been in trailer before, won't this make the anxiety less for my horse? If I start out by taking them on short rides several times before I plan on transporting him on a longer trip, will I have a calmer horse? Oh yes. Try it.

Bonding and Separation...All horses, ok maybe most horses, get very attached to one or more of their stable mates. You may wean them from their dam when they are old enough (usually five months). But if you have many horses you will from time to time be weaning the horse from their "friend" for one reason or another. This affects the horse. Think about it before you plan on separating and make it as easy as possible. Make sure you have whatever other horse you will be pairing him/her with and have them nearby for a few days. Maybe in a nearby adjoining paddock. Then it is not as traumatic that the number one buddy is moved.

Grouping Brood Mares..... Broodmares need to be friends and get along so you don't have unnecessary kicking at one another. Not good for pregnant mares. A kick in the wrong place could possibly make a mare abort. Maybe you have bred a younger mare and she needs to be introduced into the area where other broodmares are kept. Do this gradually. Maybe across the fence from one another or stalled close by. Then turn her with one of the broodmares at a time for a short time until they all appear to be accepting the "newcomer" in the group. Foaling time should be considered too. Broodmares can be a fussy group. But then again, think of all the hormonal changes that are taking place in those big bodies. Let's let them be that way. Quoting another writer...'blessed are the brood mares'

Training and Safety... Everyone who gets a horse wants to ride. Get a horse-tack up and go. Looking back, I shudder. Riding helmets, no way...that's for sissies. Tack...what's tack? Oh that's something you get from the hardware store right? Right? wrong.

A horse is a thousand pound plus animal who wants to do what he wants to do when he wants to do it. When I first started riding, we just threw the saddle upon the horse, wherever it landed had to be the right place. We put whatever bit we had, whatever it was called into the horse's mouth. We knew nothing about fit adjustment or function. Oh yes, the good Lord was looking out for us. People are injured and sometimes killed because all they had was the love or desire to buy the horse but did not seek help in approaching horse ownership or horseback riding in a knowledgeable way.

If you are just getting started, read all you can. Go to as many seminars as you can. Take riding lessons and ask lots of questions. Maintain an open mind. You will never know it all and that's what keeps it interesting. I have learned my lessons the hard way. I hope that I can pass on what knowledge I have and make you aware of my mistakes. So, hopefully, you will not make the same ones. You will make your own, but with some basic horsemanship and horseback riding instruction, you will make then safely.

Buying a Horse….and so you want to buy a horse. Many time I have telephone calls from all ages of would be horse enthusiast. Their question would be 'do you have any horses for sale'. I would answer with yes and then ask them what they were looking for. You would be surprised at some of the questions I am asked, but the ones I really love are the ones from children. They may say they want a black horse or maybe a white horse. All they know is they want a horse. I spend a lot of time with whomever calls. Hopefully they will be our future horse owners. If it is an adult you should want to guide them the right way. It is well worth the time.

I start off by telling them not to be in a hurry to purchase a horse. TAKE YOUR TIME. It is real easy to get caught up in the excitement of looking and falling in love with the first one you come in contact with. Look at several. Visit lots of farms. Then ask yourself, which one fits your pocket book/budget. Which one has a calm disposition, which one has adequate training. Then narrow the list down. Go back to that particular farm more than one time to see and try the horse. Watch the horse be groomed, tacked up, lunged then ridden. Try to go back when the farm owner is not expecting you.

Next step would be to have the horse Vet-checked for soundness. This is money well spent. Then unless you are 100% sure that this is a good horse for you and or your child ask about lease/purchase agreement. Horse would be insured for sale price. This protects seller and buyer. You pay for that.

You would provide full maintenance on the horse such as veterinarian expenses, farrier expenses, etc. Then an agreement between you and seller on the amount you would pay per month/ two to six months. At any time during that lease if horse should not be the one for you lease is terminated and you forfeit monthly payments. When you have decided that this is the horse for you, the lease payments go towards sale price of horse.

Some sellers may balk at this suggestion, but in almost all cases when we have been involved with this lease/purchase the horse sells itself. The bond that takes place between horse and rider seals the deal.

I would think that no one, and I mean no one, would want to sell a horse particularly for a child that would not be in the best interest of the child.

By the way…..there is no such thing as a child proof horse.

JAZABELLE, APACHE, AND MOLLY

Holy Moly, Horse Trading

I love telling stories on myself, instead of someone else telling on me.

During my young adult life we had really jumped in over our heads and bought two riding horses. Horses we knew nothing about.

One was a beautiful black mare and I named her Jazabelle. The kids and I were able to ride her with no problems. Except for the fact she decided one day to take me over a cattle guard. Woops, we made it.

The other one we bought we named Apache. A big bold dun colored gelding that had a great disposition. He did have a fault, when you rode him, you could not stop him. Usually a correct bit will stop a horse. Sometimes it may take more. For Apache, no bit helped. Turning him in circles slowed him down, but did not stop him. We finally sold him because I was afraid the kids would get hurt on him. By the way whoa didn't work either.

So after buying these two horses from this "horse dealer", the man began telling me about this mare he had that was "in foal". Whoa again…a mare in foal!!

He showed this mare to me and even though she was skin over bones, literally, he assured me that if I would go to a bakery and get 'day old' bread and feed it to her along with her regular feed she would pick up her weight just fine. Sure…and also she was only $100.00 That is one hundred dollars. At that time my monthly salary was $350.00 a month. Here I paid one hundred dollars for a sack of bones, but oh yes, a mare in foal. How lucky. One hundred dollars was a lot of money. I think he let me pay it in four installments. Wow. What a deal..

I couldn't resist. Bought the mare and began the fattening process. Right? Right. All the bread, feed and dewormers did not help this poor mare named Molly. A few months after trying these tips for weight gaining, the mare stayed the same. Skin and bones. I finally had the veterinarian check to see if for sure she was in foal and YEP you guessed it. She was not in foal and never had been.

Molly got progressively worse and ultimately had to be put down. Poor skinny Molly, that we had come to love bones and all. But we couldn't let her suffer.

This lesson is in our 'one to remember' list regarding horse traders/dealers. My advice is to know with whom you are dealing. Ask yourself a few things. How long has this person been in the horse business? What is the condition of his animals? Condition of his premises? Ask around to see if anyone you know has had any business dealings with them.

That is why, I REPEAT. don't get in a hurry when in the market for a horse. Don't fall in love with the first one you see.

SKHAR

Scar, Scarf, 'Whats in a Name"...

Gus and I had been married for at least five years and lived in the country. We had a shed row barn that had remained empty and a fenced area. Horses hadn't even been brought into the picture up till this time. We had other hobbies that kept us busy and on the road. Didn't need anything at home that needed care.

Up until this time, I had not owned horses for a very, very long time.

While attending a shooting competition, a friend announced to all present that his Arabian mare had just foaled a filly. My husband's expression perked up.

Yes, Gus did perk up when he heard Arabian filly because he had been exposed to the Arabian breed when he was in the Culver Academy Black Horse Troup. He became aware that the Arabian horse was "people friendly". Also he talked about their intelligence, animation, and versatility. Arabian horses are sometimes referred to as the 'versatile Arabian'.

History has told us how the Bedouin tribes actually had their horses in the tents, their homes. The horse was so important to their survival that they were kept very close. Without the horse they could not fight their enemies, gather their food or move from place to place. History also tells us that great leaders fought their enemies riding the Arabian horse, most of the time using mares.

A story told, whether fiction or truth I do not know, that five mares had just endured a long battle with very little food and water and they had just returned to camp. The horses were untacked and released to go to the pool of water quite a way off.

Suddenly the enemy was again approaching and the head horseman sounded the horn of battle. The mares immediately turned around and returned to their masters. Still in need of food and water when they were called back. Their faithfulness was stronger than their physical needs.

Gus' family had cattle ranches so in the summer time it was necessary for him to work at the ranches and spend a lot of time on horseback. Their horses were not necessarily pets. They were a necessary part of ranch work.

He tells the story about how the horses were just left alone with no training until they were about five or six years old. At that time they were rounded up, put in pens, roped, saddled and with some gutsy cowboy on its back who rode it bucking all the way until it calmed down. Then they considered it broke. Yes broke. Back in those days when they wanted to get a horse ready for someone to use for work they literally broke the spirit of the horse. That horse, they thought, knew who the boss was.

Even to this day, I detest that phrase. I prefer to hear someone say the horse has been trained. Trained to be handled, trained to trust you as a friend and trained to be ridden. I truly believe that this begins as soon as the foal is born. You can truly appreciate the fact that it begins that day and from then on every time you touch or do anything with and to the horse you are teaching it "something". Hopefully good habits and not bad.

Now let's go back to that conversation about the Arabian filly that had just been born. Gus' eyes lit up and even though he denies it to this day, he said to me "we might have to get that filly". I was shocked. There was more conversation with our friend. Where was the filly? How much did he want for her? When could we get her? Oh my, let the fun begin.

We were told that she was still on her mother and that when she was weaned they would have her transported. This was in September and sometime in December she would be six months old.

I was so excited. I really had not mentioned having a horse even though we had acreage and a barn. Just hadn't thought about it YET. Got that? I am sure sooner or later horses would have been brought up.

December rolled around and we were notified that "she" would be arriving soon. We made ready for our beautiful Arabian filly's arrival. When that day came and she was taken out of the trailer, I thought she was the most beautiful horse I had seen. Boy looking back, was I blind?

All of you horse owners can probably relate to this….I never met a horse I didn't like and then this purebred filly comes along.

Up until that time, I had nothing to compare to this filly. I had owned mature horses in my young adult life but never a young one. How was I to know that she had a big fat belly because she was wormy or that her long winter coat made her look like a donkey and her awkward size made her look muley. She looked like an Arabian princess to me. How lucky I was to have such a treasure.

Going back to my "not knowing anything about horses "era. I purchased things I thought I needed, such as grooming products and her feed. Now what should I feed her? I thought by reading directions on the feed bag would be enough information. Guess it was ok, because we didn't kill her by overfeeding.

We gave her a few days to settle in before calling my

veterinarian, Dr. Sherwood for a routine check. When I talked on the telephone with him his first question was did I get a negative Coggins test with her? A what? He began to explain to me that a Coggins test was a test for swamp fever (Equine Infectious Anemia) Something all horse people should know about and definitely have a negative test on a horse when bought. Whatever was needed at this time for my beautiful filly I would have Dr S do.

A few days later Dr. S came to the ranch and did a physical on the filly, all of which was normal. He gave me a paste dewormer with instructions as to when it should be repeated. He also gave her all the immunization injections she needed at this time and drew blood from her for the Coggins test. This blood would be sent to Texas A & M University Veterinarian hospital laboratory.

A week or so later I received a telephone call from Dr. S telling me that the lab work showed the test to be positive for swamp fever. And just what that means, I asked him? He proceeded to tell me that this was a very contagious equine disease that could not be cured. If a horse showed to be positive he or she must either be destroyed (euthanized) or quarantined quite a distance from other horses FOREVER.

I was dumbfounded and I started to cry. I have had my beautiful filly for only one month and found out that she had an incurable disease and probably needed to be destroyed. I couldn't think straight so I told Dr. S that I would call him back.

As I said earlier, I knew nothing about horses. So many people even now buy horses and don't know anything about them or their care.

You can mention negative Coggins to a potential horse owner and many times they have no idea what you are talking about.

Skhar, 6 months

Skhar, 2 years old

Jean riding Skhar with no tack

After a while, I called Dr. S back and asked him if there could possibly be a mistake? He said he didn't think so...these tests were always correct as far as he knew. I asked if he would redraw the blood and send it anyway and he agreed. In the meantime I contacted the previous owner who still had the mare and he likewise was shocked.

He told me he would have the mare checked and let me know.

I can't tell you how upset I was and discouraged to say the least.

Within one week after sending in second specimen I received a letter from the laboratory and it read something like this. 'We hope we have not caused you any undue anxiety but there was a mistake in the previous lab report'. The report was negative.

What if I had immediately put the filly down"? Lesson learned -don't take this test or the results lightly. It is important that we continue to be vigilant on testing our horses on a regular basis. Yearly.

I have had people tell me their horses never leave their homes, why should they have their horses tested? You never know when someone will be coming to your place with a horse for one reason or another. You should always be ready to transport your horse (particularly from one state to another) whether it be for competition or a trip to the veterinary hospital. Most states require this test when crossing state line.

This disease has declined tremendously since the Coggins Test came into existence in the 1970s. Part of the reason for the decline is strict state laws, equine rules and regulations for events.

Please note: one of the first things you must ask a potential seller is whether or not this horse has a current negative Coggins test, along with current immunizations.

Now back to my filly. By the time I got through this Coggins thing

I began to realized I really didn't know anything about horses. The time had come to attend seminars, read books and articles on horse ownership and to pick my veterinarian's brain. Forty plus years later, I am still doing the same thing.

This first filly was named SKHAR. We relied on the previous owner to name her since we were not familiar with Arabian horses names. Boy we have been through many names by this time. SKHAR he said, meant ammunition. Over the years SKHAR has been called and pronounced many, many ways. What's in a name?

When SKHAR was a little over a year old, she blossomed into a beautiful young filly. We thought she might be good enough for halter showing so we contacted a young trainer that we loved and trusted.

He and his wife came to the ranch and before we took him out to see SKHAR we had lunch and visited a while. I brought out pictures of SKHAR as she was when she first arrived at the ranch. We sat back to watch the expression of our potential trainer. He never showed any emotion to the muley, fuzzy, wormy looking filly. We wanted to burst out laughing. What a bad trick to play on him. We then showed photos of how she looked at this time. What a difference. To this day we raze him about that day and he just laughs. The customer is always right.

Right?

We won't go into whether or not SKHAR made it as a National Champion. It was, however, the beginning of a wonderful friendship and partnership with many horses in training with this young man.

SKHAR let us know when she was quite young that the show ring was not for her. Anytime she was shown under saddle, particularly with an amateur, she would cut the corners short and almost run over the judge. Not literally, but it sure looked that way.

SKHAR preferred being a stay at ranch broodmare. She also turned out to be a great lesson horse. Her wonderful disposition was just what the new rider needed for confidence. She was one of the mounts used at our equine summer camps.

She could also be ridden without any tack. I enjoyed that a lot. If she didn't stop with WHOA I would stretch my legs around her chest and she would stop. A sweety.

At the start of this "book" SKHAR was thirty one years old and still being used for lessons. She had reverted back to the fuzzy looking little horse she was as a six month old. Older, wiser and sweet as ever.

I can't tell you how many people experienced learning to ride on SKHAR. People all ages and from all walks of life.

SKHAR was thirty-two years old when she went to the greener pastures.

SKHAR was truly missed when she no longer roamed around the ranch.

SKHAR's dam lived to be thirty eight years old.

BLESSED ARE THE BROOD MARES (OUR MARES)

Ready to Foal...

Off and on I have related stories about some of the mares here at the ranch and some of the foals being born that I attended. If you are an owner of a brood mare over a period of time there are different things you may encounter in trying to get your mare in foal and keep her in foal. In most cases you probably won't have any problems but sometimes they need a little help.

Keep the mare content...don't make any changes in her daily routine, such as taking her away from her stable mate. Plan ahead. Keep the mares you are going to breed together. Hopefully they will get in foal and have their foal in about the same time frame. If you have just one horse, just don't make too many changes in her routine.

For thousands and thousands of years, along with other animals in the wild, horses have reproduced without any interference from humans. If they were not strong, they would not survive and surely if their foals were not strong and healthy, they would not survive. So with our domestic horses we feel we can do a better job, breeding and foaling...

yes we can.

Mares and foals

Shwikar just foaling

Shwikar/Pami

Most breeders want their mares bred so that they foal sometime in January. The reason for this is, come the next January 1 the foal is considered a year old, regardless of the month in which it was born.

If your foal is in a two year old futurity and it was born in May or June, it is still considered a two year old. That second year, Jan 1 needless to say this two year old would not be as mature as the ones born earlier in the year. This is really an important factor in the race horse industry.

As for me, it is not important for the foal to be born in the cold early months. Instead I prefer breeding my mares so that they would foal in March or later. If you are the one out in the cold all night until the wee hours of the morning you too may consider when you breed your mare.

Gestation for the horse is eleven months, at least that's what the books all say and that gives you an estimated date to realllllllly be watching the mare for signs of foaling in the near future.

Two or three weeks before estimated due date, start looking over your mare. You are looking for changes in several areas. The udder, does it appear to be getting fuller? Are the nipples changing? Start watching for waxing. You may see a little at a time, maybe a lot all of a sudden, maybe dripping milk, or maybe none of the above.

What about the gland that runs underneath her abdomen. This is a gland that becomes enlarged to some extent. (the milk gland) Now observe her hips. Are they sagging somewhat and loose? The vulva, is it looking relaxed and droopy?

These are what I say are obvious changes in the mare prior to her "close" foaling time. When you notice these changes and she really, really looks close to her time, she may do some rolling. She is getting that foal in position….Getting closer

FOALING AROUND

Foaling preparation check list that we used here at ranch.

1}   Observe mare daily AM & PM

2}   All items needed for foaling are in foaling box. (Iodine, fleet enema dental floss. In case cord does not break the floss is to be tied to usual breaking point of cord then cut. Iodine to follow.

Have available outside stall:
hay
bucket for placenta
towels
manure bucket and rake
two grocery bags and hay string

4}   Foaling stall recleaned in PM. (every day)

5}   Baby buzzer put on every evening. Also in day time if symptoms indicate foaling could be soon. ♥Be sure and turn transmitter off when it is taken off in the A.M. *Always check transmitter to be on and working before putting it on mare. It won't do any good if it doesn't send a signal to alert you as to the upcoming foal.*

When mares are nearing their due date one must check the overall condition of the mare from day to day. Check her teats a.m. and p.m. you will be surprised at the difference in bagging up, waxing, dripping, etc., from a.m. to p.m. Nearing foaling the teats will be large, engorged and tight. Under the belly (midline) you will gradually see the milk gland become enlarged.

The abdomen will be droopy and the hips relaxed and dropped. The vulva will be very relaxed.

"NOW MIND YOU" this can occur for hours--days--or longer before foaling. Just keep watching and waiting. This is where your patience pays off. They will not foal until time is right.

EARLY STAGES OF LABOR:

Restlessness, mare up and down. Sweating, defecating often, moving about stall a lot. Mare will sometime tease to a stallion that might be near her paddock. I assume the hormones are very confused at this time.

Other symptoms--mare will lie down flat and then at times semi-flat and look at her abdomen.

When she is in the final stages of labor, trying to break the water amniotic fluid she will usually lay flat out and with stiff legs and begin to strain. You may confuse urine to the amniotic fluid. The pressure of the foal on the bladder area will cause urine to seep out--be assured when the "water breaks" it will be like a small flood. You will *know the difference*.

Almost immediately, one hoof should appear, then another hoof, and then the nose of the foal (resembling a diving position). *If after water breaks,* mare is still straining and you do not see the hooves and nose appear--you may see the anus being pushed out and upward by these hooves and this is not good. Hooves can perforate through the rectal wall and cause considerable damage. Get mare up--(halter and rope and someone holding her) gently slip your hand into the upper part of the vagina and feel for the hooves. Usually just a gentle guidance with your hand, they will come on out. Then get out and leave mare alone. If you are alone and this happens, wait until the mare lies down and do the same thing, speaking quietly and gently to build her confidence in you.

Sometime when hooves do present, they are upside down---again make mare get up and _usually_ when she lies back down, the hooves are correct and the foal in correct position. IF NOT CALL THE VETERINARIAN RIGHT AWAY.

VERY IMPORTANT; leave mare alone and observe her undetected when she starts into labor. If you have several people joining you for this event, make sure they are watching in area so the mare cannot see them. If disturbed--mare can and will put off the event for as long as possible. You want her calm at this time--not nervous. You want her trusting--not fearful.

Check list:

Mare has most of the symptoms we spoke of earlier:

a. Abdomen dropped
b. Hips loose and dropped
c. Milk gland under belly enlarged (maybe)
d. Vulva relaxed
e. Teats engorged
f. Sometime teats waxing (colostrum)
g. Sometimes dripping milk

When these symptoms are apparent (many or most) wrap mare's tail with ace bandage.(Note: when bathing the mare days before foaling is expected--_do not_---I repeat,--do not use showsheen on tail. (Tail wrap will not stay in.) Not everyone will put on tail wrap.

Other things to do on the "days" you are just sure she will foal..... groom the mare thoroughly. If mare is shedding a lot of her coat, when foal is trying to find the faucet department, the loose hair around the abdomen and teats is annoying to the foal and it will give you trouble trying to get the foal to nurse. Along with the grooming you should wash the teats and the vulva area.

Mare, unaware of watchful eyes, is very restless, defecating often. Lying down, getting up. Looking at her sides. Finally she lays flat out, straining--fluid comes--remember could be urine--then finally water breaks. Mare may get up and down several times even after the two hooves and nose have appeared. The hooves may come out a little way, then go back in. This is O.K. Don't get excited........

HOWEVER-----if water does break and after 5--10--15 minutes you see nothing call Veterinarian immediately. Put halter and rope on mare and get her up. Try to calm her. She will still want to lie down and strain. If no hooves or nose appear keep trying to get her up. You may have to do this until veterinarian arrives.

If presentation is correct--one hoof--second hoof--then nose. Leave the mare alone. I repeat *leave her alone* and **STAY OUT OF SIGHT.** When foal is out (rear feet may still be inside her) the sac has torn off the foal's nose and foal is breathing, leave them alone. If the sac is still over the foal's nose then you *must* go in quietly and tear the sac from across the foal's nose so it may breath. **OTHERWISE LEAVE THEM ALONE.**

As long as the umbilical cord is attached, blood is being passed from the placenta to the foal. This is important. **LEAVE THEM ALONE.**

While mare and foal are lying there quietly, it is time for you to make a hot bran mash for mare. My receipt:

1 and 1/2 pound bran
1/2 pound sweet feed

4 - 6 tablespoons table salt

3/4 cup of Karo syrup (approx.)

Add enough hot water and stir so it is the consistency of thick cooked cereal. Let stand 3 to 5 minutes covered. ...then quietly, calmly, speaking softly to mare--put the hot bran mash which has been prepared in a <u>small</u> bucket, in front of the mare so she can eat it while she is still lying down. If she accepts it and eats everything is on course. This is not only my own personal opinion, Hansi Heck, long time breeder and friend believed it too. ***LEAVE THEM ALONE--THIS IS A BONDING TIME***

Foal may move about and try to stand, the mare may get up. During one of these times, umbilical cord ***<u>SHOULD</u>*** break. At this time preferably one person --unless you feel you need help-- should go in and cauterize naval stump with iodine . I use plastic holder that syringe comes in. You will see that it is easier to guide the naval stump into it for cauterization.

There have been times when the umbilical cord did not break and pinching it in the usual breakage area did not work. This is where the dental floss comes in.

Umbilical tape or dental floss is used to tie the cord in the area where it should break after cutting. Dip stump into iodine. Cord used to tie stump should be removed the next day. Be sure and cauterize three days in a row

When mare gets up, put halter and rope on her. She will get upset if you keep her away from foal. Keep her nose with foal. You will need someone to help now. Use two double grocery bags (plastic) and hay string and put the sac and umbilical cord, etc. into these bags and tie it up to her tail as high as possible and close to vulva. This weight will help the mare expel the placenta. If the mare should step on the dragging sac, and the sac tear off, you will not have this weight to assist the release of the placenta.

When the placenta is expelled use the bucket you have nearby in the hallway. Take the placenta into the hallway (near an area that can be washed down after its examination) lay it out on the floor and check it thoroughly for any tears other than the one tear where the foal broke out. Sometimes the placenta expels inside out (inverted). The color and the blood may alarm you. Just turn it right side out. If you have any doubts as to whether the placenta is intact or not, save it and show it to the Veterinarian.

After foal has gotten up on its feet (and this can take anywhere from 15 minutes and *longer*), a fleet enema that has been sitting in warm water should be given to foal *regardless* as to whether or not it has passed any feces. When inserting tip of enema do so slightly up. After the enema is given in 5-10 minutes foal will pass the meconium. **Be sure and watch for this to occur.**

Prior to foaling, mare was friends or acquaintance with mare next door -- **NOW** -- after foaling, she doesn't even want the other mare to look at her. You may have to put up additional cover between mare and foal's stall and the nearest neighbor. Otherwise, mare will be nervous and won't stand still for foal. All of these ideas relate to the fact that you must think about what the mare is feeling. Particularly when the mare is a maiden mare.

NURSING

The remaining important thing for the foal to do, is nurse. This needs to be left to mare and foal to work out if at all possible. No interference.

Sometimes if milk is not flowing, you may have to milk each teat a small amount in order to get the milk started.

Many times the foal will act like it is interested in nursing but isn't. When you really notice the foal making sucking sounds and trying to nurse everything around, wall included, then the foal is ready to nurse. Before that you are wasting your time if you try and make it nurse. Foal _must_ nurse adequate colostrum (milk). Do not take for granted that is looks like the foal is nursing, be sure.

Give the mare and foal as much time as you feel is necessary alone without "you" being there where she can see you. Let them work out the nursing if at all possible.

Steps to take if and when they can't work it out.

1. Halter mare and hold her quietly, let her nuzzle foal. Gently push foal to teat area. Nursing for a maiden mare is sometime a little more difficult. It should be made a pleasant experience when you are handling her. ***Do not fuss at her, be gentle!***
2. Milk the mare, put milk on teats to aid the foal in finding the faucets.
3. If mare is resistant to the foal trying to nurse she may be tender or even in pain from foaling. Apply a shoulder twitch and then let foal try to nurse. If shoulder twitch is not strong enough then nose "humane" twitch, just for the first nursing, only as a last resort.
4. In some cases, Ace Promazine can be given to mare. Ask your veterinarian.

If these methods do not work, call veterinarian and let him advise you. Unless you are experienced handling this situation you will make matters worse by trying to force this important part of mare/foal relationship.

O.K.-Final check list

To this point you should have:

1. Foal born without complications.
2. Hot bran mash to mare.
3. Cauterized navel stump with iodine after cord breaks.
4. Fleet enema to foal - meconium passed.

5. Foal has nursed.
6. Placenta passed (checked).

When mare may retain the placenta for longer than usual. She will continue to have contractions and shows signs of discomfort.. Many times she will not be interested in her foal. If the placenta has not passed in 2 hours call your veterinarian. He may tell you to give oxytocin. Go from there.

After steps 1 -6 (above) have been done:
1. Give mare 10cc Banamine IM
2. Give mare 20 cc Dipyrone IM
*IM - Intramuscularly.

Again, this is and was what our veterinarian had prescribed us to administer back then..

Continue to observe mare and foal to make sure they are both alert, eating good; and that foal is having normal bowel movements.

For the next three days continue to cauterize the naval stump. ***Do not guess about anything!***

FOAL REJECTION

A Second Chance...

If you are a breeder of horses, it is just a matter of time before you will experience "foal rejection".

Our case involved a maiden mare who, after foaling, would not have anything to do with her foal trying to nurse. She wanted nothing to do with him period. No nuzzling, licking, etc. She would squeal, kick out and push him away. This was another reason being on hand at foaling became important. We first tried being patient with the mare. We tried a mild shoulder twitch, while we guided the foal to teats, talking and trying to convince her that this would get easier if she cooperated. No way, so next we tried mild tranquilizer with the shoulder twitch and verbally soothing her to accept the foal. Nope, no way. Sooooo then we got aggressive, ear twitch, nose twitch, and this too made matters worse. Still no nursing.

We all know that the colostrum is critical to the survival of the foal. Nurturing from the mare nuzzling, licking, etc., is also necessary and this was not happening. With a lot of resistance from the mare and our persistence, we milked the mare and bottle fed the foal. Because of the mare's aggressive behavior towards the foal we were not able to leave him in stall with her.

We tried working with mare and foal all day without success. Again and again we milked the mare and bottle fed the foal.

Over the next two days we kept a close eye on the foal and witnessed the depression and listless behavior. We checked the foal's temperature and it was elevated. Something had to be done if we were to save the foal. I decided we needed to get this foal on another nursing mare.

Shwikar's, one of our other brood mares had a foal old enough for us to wean so I decided we needed to start our plan for transferring our rejected foal to this mare.

Shwikar and her foal were put in stall next to our little "orphaned" foal.

Smell (odor) I know is a bond between a mare and her foal. If we had kept the placenta from Shwikar's foal we could have used it to rub on the orphan so she would think he belonged to her.

What else could we use? For whatever reason I remembered we had a small bottle of spirits of spearmint. What if I rubbed this aroma all over foal, then somehow get Shwikar to relate to it. We put a halter on Shwikar and wrapped small washcloths on each side of the halter. We then saturated them with the spearmint aroma.

Shwikar was not upset about us moving her foal who was ready to wean and for a little while we left "orphan" in stall next to her.

Now mind you, this was just an experiment. We were hopeful but not assured we would be successful transferring the foal to another mare.

We held mare and someone brought in orphan foal…Shwikar remained calm but foal was apprehensive. "Was this the mean mare that mistreated me?" "Would she kick at me or try to bite me" None of this happened. The foal kept trying to avoid his hopefully, new mom. Shwikar never, never showed any sign of being upset or confused.

During this time we stroked Shwikar and talked calmly working to convince her that all was well. We took our time, hoping and praying that this swap would work and that we would save this little guy. Slowly we guided him to the fountain of life, (especially for him.) With time and patience he began to nurse and Shwikar was calm as could be. This was her foal, at least he sure smelled like he was.

All the steps we took with the wonderful scent of spearmint worked. I will not give all credit to that aroma.....We were working with a beautiful, kind, patient Egyptian mare. That was the biggest ingredient.

Woops, did I say Egyptian Mare? This is same Mare you read about in "Placentia Previa Birth/ Red Bag. An exceptional mare to say the least.

Another Example:

We were out of town when our second foal was to be born here on the ranch to beautiful Dal Malouma. Remember we had such bad luck with our first foal, even though we ultimately saved her. Anyway, we received a phone call from the ranch that she had indeed foaled but was very nervous, going in circles in stall and would not stand for foal to nurse. Everyone at ranch was very upset. I commented to my husband, Gus, that if we wanted to save this foal, we needed to go home immediately. We cancelled the remainder of the trip and headed home that very evening.

When we got home I went to the back barn (our old shed row back then) and observed the mare. I saw immediately that mosquitos were swarming. Couldn't my help have noticed this. Weren't the mosquitos after them too.

So I right away wiped the mare down with cool wet towels speaking ever so gently to her followed by insect spray.

She settled down after a bit and let the foal nurse who had been trying long before now to nurse only to be turned away by a mare that was desperate to get away from the mosquitos. Mystery solved….and not really that complicated. JUST OBSERVE….. see what is bothering the mare.

After that Dal Malouma and baby did just great.

PLACENTIA PREVIA BIRTH

Red Bag Birth...

I had heard of this disorder before associated with human birth. I knew it was a serious condition.

Placenta Previa (sometime referred to as "Red Bag") occurs when the foal and the placenta detach at the same time. Not a good thing to happen. This keeps the foal from receiving necessary blood flow and oxygen through its umbilical cord.

When the placenta presents first, it is most important to get that foal out as soon as possible or you will end up with a foal dead from septicemia blood poisoning caused by bacteria). You have only a short period of time to deliver the foal. It is breathing fluid at this time instead of air. (Note: Septicemia is a blood poisoning especially caused by bacteria or their toxins,)

Earlier I told you we had no monitoring devices to let us know when mare was beginning labor. Well by this time we had come up in the world. First, we bought a BABY BUZZER. This was a wonderful device. There was a surcingle attached to mare with a transmitter attached to it. Also there was a receiver we placed near phone in barn. When the mare laid flat out to sleep or to begin foaling the transmitter sent a signal to the receiver and a loud beeping sound was heard.

Red Bag

Red Sac

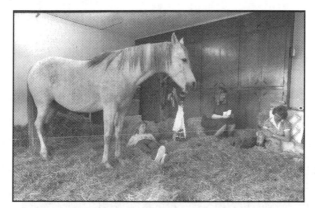

Garage Intensive Care

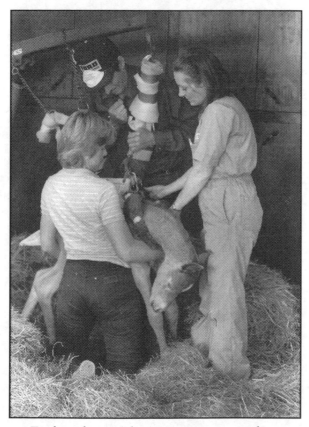

Foal in sling with veterinarian attending

Now along with the Baby Buzzer, we had a camera looking into foaling stall and the monitor was next to my bed….. in order for me to hear the beeping, the phone bedside was put on hands free to the barn. We heard the beep…and oh yes birds chirping, dogs barking and any other noise that helped you lose sleep. Some mares rarely lay flat out when they sleep and then again some lay flat quite often and this really adds to your loss of sleep. When I heard beep through the phone, I would raise up, look into monitor and see if I could tell whether or not the mare was indeed starting into labor or just getting some needed rest.

On this particular night the beeping sounded. I watched the mare to see if she was indeed about to foal…..she was.

Many a friend or family member would say to me., " when the mare starts in labor, call me." When a mare starts in labor you don't have time to make a phone call. By the time you get out to the barn, in most cases the foal is presenting. "They" could never get there in time, at least for the foaling.

When I reached the barn and peeked in, I saw this "unusual" red bag coming out. I knew immediately we had a problem and I needed to get that foal out as soon as possible. When I did get foal out, I began briskly rubbing the foal with towel. It was having problems breathing and was in a convulsive state. Finally it began to breathe "normal" and I called Dr. S. to tell him I had a problem.

On arrival Dr. S examined the foal and he knew we were in trouble. We milked the mare and bottle fed the foal. The foal was not strong enough to stand and nurse on her own. We did indeed have a problem. The weather was cold with the temperature in the 40s, but I stayed with the mare and foal until morning. I would milk mare and bottle feed the foal. In the morning we realized we needed to move to a warmer location not only for the foal and mare but for those of us that would end up staying with foal and mare around the clock.

An intensive care unit for the mare and foal was set up in the garage. Someone had to milk the mare ever so often, and keep the foal in the sternum position so she would not get pneumonia. Our veterinarian call an equine hospital in Versailles, Kentucky which is one of the top veterinary clinics in the country.

(I was familiar with clinic and veterinarian because of a previous problem with a young filly.)

Our vet talked to head veterinarian at that clinic who said, "Do not put the foal down. It's probable she will snap out of it in a few days." Supportive medications were prescribed for the foal. Keeping her from getting pneumonia was very important. A motor lift (small) and a sling made was used from time to time to put the foal in an upright position. Remember she could not hold herself up.

When she was in this sling, it was as though she were a puppet. She would try to right herself up, whiney, then slump down immediately down into the sling. It was amazing. When she knew that she was about to be fed, she would get excited and again whiney. We would milk the mare, add amino acids and whatever else the doctor had prescribed for her. I guess she heard the usual noises made in preparing the bottle.

Visualize: Double car garage, hay bales all around, mare and foal inside at night, quilts for attendant (including myself) to sit on and hold foal. At one point during my watch, I was holding the foal and she tossed her head back and guess who got a black eye.

In the daytime, the garage was open and mare was free to graze in yard. From time to time she came back to check on her foal. When she was out in yard and it was time for her to be milked, all I had to do was take my plastic Tupperware measuring cup (2 qts size which I still have) with handle, kneel beside mare and start milking. She never moved nor did she mind. I can just imagine, people driving by seeing unrestrained mare being milked by some crazy lady kneeling down beside mare with Tupperware cup. Yep, we did. Then back to the foal for her bottle.

This treatment in the intensive care garage went on for ten days with no improvement. We decided to call the vet in Kentucky and tell him that we would be sending him a video of the foal. Perhaps this would help him understand what we were dealing with.

After reviewing the video, he telephoned us and said he was so sorry. This condition was irreversible. He indicated that filly did not get sufficient oxygen at birth. He initially thought it might be Dummy Foal Syndrome/Neo Natal Maladjustment Syndrome and that can be a condition from which a foal can recover.

We chose not to euthanize the filly at the ranch. Instead we took her to LSU Veterinarian Hospital in Baton Rouge. We hoped that they might be able to learn something from her condition and help others in the future.

We all learned a lot from the 10 days that we dedicated to the care of this filly. Hope kept us going. Doesn't it always?

The foal's dam was Shiwkar, Egyptian Arabian mare that was imported from Egypt. She was the first Egyptian Arabian mare that we bought. She was a treasure and gave us many beautiful foals.

BINT FERTAMA

Thank Goodness You're Here...

Ok so you have purchased your first horse, Shkar. (that was us). If you are smart you will stop with one or two. But what's with this smart stuff. I've already described myself as being a dummy a long time ago, but that was then and this is now.

That first Arabian filly just gave us a hit of what owning Arabian horses would be like. Surely out there were many more that would be an asset to our farm. So on a trip to California to see a new grandchild, we took a side trip to an Arabian horse farm to see what we could see. Now mind you, not just any farm but an exclusive farm that number one daughter had corresponded with after reading about them in a horse magazine.

We called and made arrangements to visit the farm. We took our daughter-in-law and new grandson who was six weeks old.

We were in awe of the beauty and calmness of their horses. We went to the mare pasture and all the mares came around the baby in arms to see what this little thing might be. They literally came right up and wanted to sniff him. So friendly and personable. We had never been to a farm like this, in fact it was the first Arabian farm we visited after purchasing Skhar.

Bint Fertama and foal

Sudama out of Bint Fertama

My husband had said that the Arabian horse is known for its closeness with humans, but this was really a surprise to me to see the mares come up and pay attention to the baby.

We visited with the people at the farm for a while before we got down to business. We asked the manager to show us some of the horses that were for sale. He showed us several, well maybe just a couple, and we were quite impressed.

The first one was a big beautiful grey (white) mare who was definitely in foal. In fact, we were told that she was due to foal within the next two to three weeks. First dumb question....is she rideable? Poor mare, so big in foal, but the manager tacked her up and got on her.

Here we were looking for a brood mare and I wanted to know if she was trained to saddle.

He did tell us about her show career and that she had been a halter champion at a world class show in Scottsdale.

While the mare was still tacked up and just standing there, I asked the second dumb question. What was the asking price for this mare? Answer $25,000.00. Silence on my part. Manager had gone back to untack the mare.

Then I took a deep breath and said to my husband "twenty five thousand dollarssssss"?

My previous experience had been buying horses in the one to two hundred dollar range, so I nearly fainted behind his back at that moment.

Well, we did purchase the mare, pregnant and all and she turned out to be a great producer of champions. Many times.

The offspring of Bint Fertama that were sold, saw the horse business at it's highest and then again at its lowest.

I have many good memories with Bint Fertama. I spent many a night waiting for her to foal, and when she was ready to foal I was always there to lend a helping hand. When she was in labor and foal was presenting I would enter the stall to assist her. The look from her was "well for thank goodness, you're here".

Bint Fertama had her last foal at age 25. Yes, this is quite unusual but she did. She lived to be thirty years old.

The Old Grey Mare..... was very kind and gentle. We miss her very much.

FADAMAZE

Amazing Fadamaze, Til Death Do Us Part

The transport pulls up outside gate. The long trip for Fadamaze has ended. A tall, gaunt, thin grey mare descends the ramp, looks around and makes her arrival known.

Fadamaze was purchased, sight unseen, on the basis of her pedigree alone. Ever since we purchased our foundation brood mare, Bint Fertama my husband had become intrigued by the Fadjur bloodlines. So when he found the advertisement about Fadamaze, he called, inquired and purchased.

Unless you breed, foal and raise a horse you never really know what to expect. What type of disposition do they have? Any bad habits….any health issues…any breeding and foaling problems? You never know. You just have to have faith. Well I am not that gutsy. I like to have a hands on introduction when I am considering buying any animal, much less a horse.

I walked Fadamaze up to the barn and finished paperwork with the transporter. I then proceeded to go over Fadamaze inch by inch to see what her reactions would be to a new person and new environment. I guess if you or I had been in a transport van some 24 to 36 hours (or more) we would be placid and/or half dead too.

Fadamaze was to be part of our broodmare band so the main

thing at that time was to settle her in, get her caught up in our routine and be ready for the breeding season. At the time she arrived she was very thin. We gradually got her on a good feed and deworming program and she blossomed.

Fadamaze was a very kind and sweet mare. We had no problems getting her in foal. Now all we had to do was wait.

When time came for Fadamaze to foal, we still just had the shed row barn out back. The main barn was in early states of construction.

Unlike, in years to come, we had no closed circuit TV or foaling devices to alert us when a mare was ready to foal. The only thing we could do is what millions of horse people do year after year. Come up with a more or less expected date of foaling then wait. Watch the mare for changes in her body such as loosening in the hips, relaxed vulva, enlarged milk gland under her abdomen and the possibility of waxing.

Waxing, prior to foaling, is the formation or dripping of a thick substance called colostrum. In most cases right up before foaling, the waxing will become milk dripping. You note I said in most cases. I have had mares show slight waxing, then it goes away...more time passes, slight waxing again, might go away or might get heavier. Sometimes the first sign is only the milk dripping.

What I am trying to tell you is there "ain't no" sure sign that the mare will foal in the very near future. She will foal if and when she gets good and ready. Another thing to watch for is restlessness and the mare rolling. By rolling I mean mare gets down, rolls onto her back and in most cases rolls from side to side. Sometimes she rolls completely. She is positioning the foal.

Well back to Fadamaze. We watched for signs and the only thing we could do was go out from to time and check on her. That meant day and night. On the night that one of my employees had gone to check on her Fadamaze had just foaled.

Our employee telephoned from the barn and everyone in the house was up and out. It became immediately obvious that the foal was not breathing. Mouth to nose resuscitation was performed on the foal and the foal was rubbed vigorously. Thank God the foal began to breath. We all sighed a breath of relief thinking we were out of the woods, and everything would be o.k.

.This foal was born in the very early hours of morning. All things considered, we followed our foaling guidelines and gave Fadamaze and her foal more than enough time before one of us went back into the stall to assist.

Fadamaze with "dummy foal"

The foal had made several attempts to stand but kept falling. Some of this is normal, but in this case it was longer than usual. We attempted to assist the foal in standing but it was a struggle for both of us.

We held the foal near the mare hoping she might show some interest in looking for the faucets. She did not.

By now it was daylight and we telephoned our veterinarian and relayed the problems we were having. After what seemed an eternity, (and I have since learned after 40 years that eternity in foaling hours has a different meaning) the Vet arrived and examined mare and foal. By now the foal would stand, but would stagger around, going in circles running into objects if you didn't stop her.

The mare was milked and the foal was tubed with colostrum. The colostrum is the mare's first milk. It contains antibodies that insure immunities are passed from mare to foal. If this does not occur and the foal does not absorb these important ingredients you could end up with a foal that is not strong. The foal would not have enough immunities of its own to fight off early on infections and could die.

Some time went by and we all watched in fear as this little newborn foal kept up the abnormal behavior. All the while the beautiful, confused Fadamaze was trying to keep up with her newborn.

This was the first foal to be born here at Plum Nearly and first hand experience for us. I was in tears by this time. I told our veterinarian that if he thought the foal would not get better, maybe we should put her down.

The abnormal behavior had continued for quite some time and by now the veterinarian was alarmed by the foals lack of progress. He decided to call Texas A & M Veterinary Hospital.

He described the symptoms and behavior of the foal. The doctor at the other end of the phone said it sounds like, what is called, a "dummy foal", medically known as Neonatal Maladjustment Syndrome. He advised us to get the foal into a quiet, darkened area and to continue milking the mare and getting as much nourishment as possible to the foal. Plus he prescribed a supportive medical regime, ie amino acids, antibiotics, etc. He told us that in some cases the foal would survive. He explained one of the reasons for these types of symptoms is swelling on the brain. He also said when the swelling subsides, foal becomes normal. (in some cases)

We opened up two stalls so that a large area would be more comfortable for mare and foal and oh yes, for me. We continued watching her in the stall and it was quite some time before foal laid down to rest. Before that she was endlessly going around and around the stall.

I literally spent most of every day and all of the nights sleeping in the stall with Fadamaze and her foal. Every three hours or so I would milk the mare and bottle feed the filly. Foal would lean on me and sort of wrap her body in a strange way around my side when she nursed the bottle. She never went towards mare to nuzzle or try to find the milk source.

On the eighth day she refused to nurse from the bottle. I really became alarmed. I thought, surely we're not going to lose her now after all this effort had been made.

Shortly thereafter, she went over to her dam and began to nose around and smell. I milked Fadamaze and got milk flowing and put some on the teats so that the foal would find it easier.

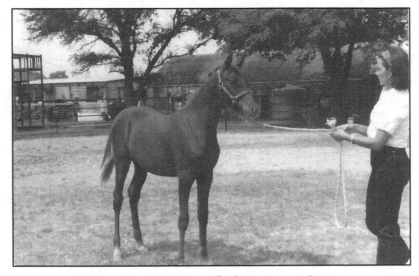

Anjur Angel (dummy foal) 1 year with Jean

It was like someone waved a magic wand and she went from "dummy foal" to a normal smart foal. We were all so excited and grateful. All the effort we had put into that baby was paying off.

From that point on she continued to do well and was a normal filly. We named the filly ANJUR ANGEL. Anjur was the name of her grand sire and the angel just came by naturally. Don't you agree?

Needless to say she was a very spoiled foal. I don't think she felt like she was a horse. She would literally run around with her nose in the air as if to say "look at me, aren't I the special one." And she really was that special. She grew into a beautiful young yearling.

Part of her early training was being taught to stand tied. One day she decided being tied was not for her so she sat back and injured one of her pasterns. She was put on oral Phenylbutazone paste. One week later she was found dead in her stall. Necropsy indicated rupture of the stomach. Medication plus ulceration of the lining of the stomach (possibly due to parasites) may have caused the rupture. Since that time I have learned that no horse should be on Phenylbutazone paste for a long period of time. That is, unless your veterinarian tell you differently.

At the time of her death, my husband and I were out of town. Someone called from the ranch to relay this information to me. I was devastated. All of us worked so hard to save this beautiful little filly who had gotten off to such a horrible start.

I learned early on that this is ownership of horses. They are big, bold, beautiful animals, but "things" happen. Just when you think you have seen it all, you ain't seen nothing yet.

Fadamaze was bred six weeks after foaling Anjur Angel to a stallion named DZ MIEKKI. The following March Fadamaze foaled twins five weeks early. One under developed and the other fully developed. Neither lived.

It is very sad when a mare foals and the foal/foals do not live. Instinct tells her baby should be there. She can smell where it has been. Where is it? She is neighing and looking. So sad. The only thing you can do is give her a mild tranquilizer and lots of love and attention. Then move her to a different location.

After the death of her twins, Fadamaze was infused with antibiotics so that her uterus would be clean and we could breed her on the six week cycle.

As before, Fadamaze got in foal and at full term foaled a filly who lived two days and died of pneumonia.

This was becoming a puzzle. The mare seemed healthy enough. She settled in pregnancy without any trouble. Yet when she foaled, the foal either did not live or had medical problems.

We took Fadamaze to one of the large animal universities and had a complete workup done to see if anything was medically wrong with the mare. Nothing was found. All reproductive organs were in good working order.

We felt at this time it would be best not to breed the mare anymore. We did not want to go through the eleven months of her pregnancy with anticipation, only to have the disappointment of an unhealthy foal.

Two years passed and we decided once again to take a chance and breed Fadamaze.

We chose a beautiful, wonderful stallion named Talisman. Beautiful grey stallion to grey Fadamaze. Grey, yet Fadamaze was white. (Grey category).

Low and behold eleven months later she foaled a big chestnut colt. The colt was healthy from the time he was born and continued to mature without problems. He had the legs and body of a runner. He and Fadamaze were always ahead of the crowd of mares and foals. We named him Talismania thinking it was a quirky name in case we decided to race him.

Race him, we did. Funny note here is when we met this wonderful gentleman in Arizona and asked him if he thought Talismania would do good racing, he said, "well he is the right color". His favorite color of race horses of course was chestnut. He did train him and raced him in California. He did pretty good.

After we brought him home to Texas we entered him in some of the "bush races" in Louisiana and believe me that was a race to see. In Louisiana, anything goes. He was joined in that race with many other breeds. It was indeed interesting.

Back to Fadamaze…we bred her back to Talisman because the two of them had produced this big and healthy foal. Again, we had no problems. From then on we continued breeding her to Talisman and all their foals were healthy foals. No problems.

Could there have been a blood factor or some other reason why other stallions bred to Fadamaze did not produce healthy foals? We may never know, but when we spoke of the long "monogamous" relationship of Fadamaze to Talisman we would remark "til death do us part".

When Talisman died we no longer bred Fadamaze. She had her last foal at age 23.

FOALS

Trial and Error/ With Hands on...

Yes that is what a new born horse is called. A foal. Usually because the gender is not yet known, or we are referring to a newborn horse in general. Or sometimes not necessarily newborn, but a very young horse.

We then call a female foal, a filly and a male foal, a colt. Some people refer to the newborn or young horse as a colt. You know whatever you want to call that precious, beautiful little horse is alright with me.

I want to tell you a few experiences that I have had over the past forty plus years dealing with foals.

I wrote in another story where our first foal to be born at the ranch was a "dummy foal" (Neonatal Maladjustment Syndrome.) And how so little we knew about horses and newborn foals at that time.

From then on it has been an exciting, rewarding and sometimes sad experience dealing with foals. So goes it in the horse world. As I said before, over the years I have learned by trial and error.

We started out not knowing how susceptible foals are to pneumonia.

When they are born, if it is in your barn/stall, you might think because there is a breeze you feel in stall, that it is o.k. for the foal.

Wrong, down where the foal is located the air is not moving. It is usually hot unless you are foaling in winter. Even then air is not moving deep down in the stall. There is ammonium odor of urine also to contend with.

So if you can make the stall so that air flows even in the bottom part of it. That would be ideal. When you are building a barn air circulation is very important to all horses. Keep that in mind.

Again if it is not winter, put in fans to circulate air.

When you transport a mare and baby to a stallion at another location, check to see where your mare and baby will be kept. How many horses are in their paddock. Is there any shade and adequate water? You might take a trip there and check on mare and foal from time to time, if possible. See how they are progressing.

This we did, and found our two mares and babies out in a paddock with many mares, intensely hot. Foals had foal heat diarrhea (which is common) but apparently their buttocks hadn't been cleaned or medicated. That wasn't as bad as the heat they were enduring with no shelter whatsoever.

Our mares had already been bred so we chose to bring them home where we would have a better handle on their care.

After we got home one foal had pneumonia and the other was having some congestion too.

We worked with our veterinarian with daily medication and even used a nebulizer on the foal with pneumonia. All this did not help and we lost the foal. After days of treatment the other foal did survive.

After that experience we decided that we would NEVER transport mare with baby to be bred. We began buying quality stallions that would compliment our breeding program.

So back to birth of a foal....Besides doing all the things necessary after they are born I also imprint the foal while it is laying quietly and has not attempted to stand. It is important that it be done right after birth. I start by rubbing foal with towel from head to tail. I begin rubbing and feeling the ears. I put my fingers gently into the ears and mouth. I rub and touch areas of the abdomen too. Legs are also rubbed and flexed if time permits. This may have to be done several times until foal is relaxed and accepting the touching. All this, along with handling the foal daily will make a big impact as you go along with his training. It has been said that imprinting is permanent and results in an unafraid but respectful foal. All the way to training under saddle the horse has trust in you. The most important part of training is trust..

We begin the first day out with the mare by putting halter on foal and holding it chest and rump as it follows her, reluctantly, out the stall.

Before releasing the foal (without halter) we rub our hands all over the foal starting with head, ears, body, legs.

From that day on everything you do to or with the foal is teaching it something. Either good or bad so pay attention to what you are doing.

After a week or two we leave the halter on the foal for a couple of hours each day. Making sure halter fits and stays in place. We sometime have to make a brow band to keep it in place.

When we groom the mare we also gently groom the foal with soft brush. If it is summer time and you have a place where you can secure the mare and allow the foal to be loose by her side safely, bathe the mare and let foal get familiar with the water.

Start at its feet with gentle flowing water and gradually let water be on foal. No major baths at this time.

We have handled and lifted the legs to pat and rub hooves, so by six weeks foal will allow hooves to be trimmed. Also by now foal is leading along side of mare with no problem.

Thinking back to the beginning when we realized how little we knew the health and well-being of a foal. On one occasion we visited with another large and well managed ranch and In talking with their breeding and foaling manager he told me one of the things he did was to body clip the foals to make them cooler.

Well, yes we began doing that and it really helped. Foals didn't seem to mind the process. We would clip a while then let foal rest before beginning again. The mare standing by and eating her hay. End result—cooler foal. Less sweating. Less respiratory problems.

When we noticed foal trying to eat with mare, we would put a creep feeder in the stall so there would be feed whenever foal wanted it. Do not put out large amounts of food, so when feed is left over, don't leave old feed in feeder. Take it out and put in fresh feed. By the time the foal is weaned it is consuming quite a bit of feed. Usually about a pound each morning and evening.

Another training exercise we used was to tie mare in stall, with rope high so that foal would not get tangled in it. Then we tied foal next to her starting with a short time and one of us standing by.

We gradually lengthened the time, while we were still in the barn nearby, and let foal get used to being tied.

So by weaning time, we have a foal halter trained and leading quietly.

A foal who is eating enough feed on its own, being bathed, and having its feet cleaned and trimmed regularly. We also have a foal that will stand tied. About this time foal is brought to areas where we are working with other horses to stand tied for quite some time. If a horse walker is available, now would be the time to teach it to walk on walker. Always put a calm horse in front of it when you first start so they will have an example. Don't tie or attach to the walker at first. Slip a rope through loop and walk along side.

There are so many things you can do to have a healthy foal. It ONLY takes time, patience and lots of TLC.

Many horse owners have a mare in foal. She foals on her own with or without complications and foal is not touched until owner finally begins training process with a fearful, distrusting horse and frustrated owner. A little different from when you start as soon as they are born with the hands on program.

Hands on…..you won't be sorry.

AMIRA CLE

Do All You Can and Hope For a Miracle...

I mentioned in some of the other mare experiences that "things happen" and we have no control whatsoever. We may try to intervene. A little something might help. But, in most cases we are interfering in "what is meant to be—is meant to be".

A beautiful chestnut mare, Donna Juanita, had been checked in foal, and on or about her third month she began to drip milk. Not waxing, milk. I talked with Dr. S and he said she was probably trying to abort. We could put her on progesterone but it probably would not help but would not hurt either.

The dripping milk continued for some time then it stopped. Maybe we were out of the woods. Maybe our little progesterone intervention helped.

Donna Juanita went full term. She went into labor in middle of the day and we were in attendance. A filly was born, very small, and at this time there seemed to be no complications.....placenta followed within a very short reasonable time.

Shortly after the placenta delivered the mare laid down. She seemed to be very uncomfortable. We thought she might be colicky. She then began to strain and before you know it another foal comes out. A very, very small foal and stillborn. It looked as though it had been dead for some time. Wow...think back about seven months Donna Juanita had tried to abort. One of the twins she was carrying was not going to live. Instead of nutrition going to one foal, it was going to two.

The first foal was very weak and could not stand without assistance. Dr. S. came and tubed the filly with colostrum. We did all the usual things after a foal is born. Both placentas were passed but Dr. S. thought it would be wise to infuse the uterus with antibiotics and said to do this for the next three days.

Since filly was so weak we stayed close and milked Donna Juanita, (who could have cared less) and we bottle fed the filly often. We continued helping her stand and by the end of the day she could stand alone but was down in her pasterns big time. We kept her stalled for the next three or four days until she was stronger.

This was the most delicate, beautiful filly with a tiny muzzle and big eyes. She looked to be a bay in color. Time would tell. Because of the complications her dam had in hanging onto twin foals and the fact that she survived despite it all....we felt a good name for her would be AMIRA which means princess and add CLE (all foals sired by the great Amir Fa Serr either had the prefix Amir before a colts name or Amira for the fillies....so....the filly being born alive was indeed a miracle.. spelled AMIRACLE.

I cannot describe how tiny this filly was. Her muzzle would fit in the palm of your hand cupped tightly. You could carry her in your arms without any struggle whatsoever.

During this time we had leased a small amount of acreage adjacent to our back paddocks and barn. There was lots of grass in this pasture so it was perfect to turn out the mares and babies during the day. We fed our mares three times a day so they would continue to make lots of milk for their foals. At lunch time the back gates were opened and the mares with babies by their sides all came to back barn to be fed. All the mares came and even

Donna Juanita came. Where was her foal, it was not following.....
One of my dear friends, Paul, went out in the pasture to where the filly was standing "oh so still" looked down and one of her legs was broken and dangling middle of cannon bone. How did this happen? Did she step in a hole? Or were her bones fragile from not getting all the needed nourishment while in the womb? This was unfixable. Our little miracle had to be put down. She was only two months old. She just wasn't meant to survive.

Mother Nature tried to warn us early on and we didn't want to accept the warning signs. Even so, if you are indeed a dedicated horse person, each and every time a problem presents itself, you must, and you will make every effort to help.

MACHO/ MACHISSIMO

Make Mine a Water...

Let's go back to one of the evenings when we were watching a mare who appeared to be ready to foal soon. Sure, very near future. The time had come and we were watching the mare in an area close by but hidden so the mare would be unaware she was being observed. This was a maiden mare and we didn't want to upset her.

The mare had been restless, then her water had broken. The foal presented normally, one foot, then another foot and nose. Great. I eased into the stall, all the while talking very low and calming to the mare. She knew I was there to help, if help was needed. After foal was completely out and the sac off its head, I slipped out of the stall to let mare and foal bond.

A bit later I slipped back in and towel dried the foal. I completed my usual imprinting routine on him. Yes, him, a big healthy colt. We named him Machissimo. Also. at that time, the naval was cauterized. Ok, so back out of the stall and let well enough be done. Ha

In a short while the colt stood and was moving around the stall. We waited for placenta to come out and of course, for the foal to nurse. That is soooooo important. You can't just assume that he will nurse and get the, oh so important, colostrum.

He moved all around the stall, sucking against the walls. After some time he was at the mare trying to find the faucets. No luck. The foal went to automatic water and started to drink. I really didn't think this could be bad. He drank water then was no longer interested in looking for milk.

Well, were we, or was I stupid to let that happen? He needed to be hungry and empty to even think about looking for milk. A lot of time passes and finally with our help he began to nurse the mare.

After 24 hours, one of the laboratory test we get on the newborns is an IGg test. The foal's blood is drawn and sent to lab to make sure he received adequate antibodies through the colostrum. Machissimo's report was good. Anytime the lab report indicates that inadequate antibodies from the colostrum were not received, a serum transfusion is indicated. Even though Machissimo got to the water first he did get an adequate amount of colostrum and it was absorbed.

Over the 45 years that we have had many foals born at Plum Nearly Ranch. Most of these foals did receive adequate antibodies from the colostrum. If not, the transfusion was necessary. The test results if ok assures you that they are more likely to be able to ward off infections.

Water or no water, Machissimo came through with flying colors.

Definition IGg

Test to measure the amount of gamma globulins within the foal's bloodstream to estimate if an "adequate" quantity of immunoglobulins has been ingested and absorbed by the foal. Test measures the gamma globulin concentrations within the bloodstream.

NEW TRICKS

Lessons Learned/ Memory...

I've always said that you should read as much as possible and attend seminars even though sometimes you think, oh my, I have heard this information before. And then one day you may experience a problem that can be solved by that memory from way back when.

It really doesn't matter how educated you may be, or how smart you think you are. Always keep an open mind and absorb any bits of information that may come in handy at one point in your life.

One "normal" day at the ranch, if there is such a thing, I noticed one of the ranch hands rushing back into the tool barn and come out with a bolt cutter. He excitedly told me that a mare was tangled up in some fencing wire down the road in one of the paddocks.

I jumped in the four wheeler with him and we went down the road. He had gone in that direction earlier to dump the manure wagon and he saw the mare down by the fence. This was in the dead of summer with temperatures in the high 90s.

As we approached the paddock I noticed the mare right next to the fence and her hind legs had wire twisted around both of them. In all probability she had rolled in the dirt next to the fence and got herself in this predicament.

This was a very intelligent horse. She was lying very still as if to say…"would someone please help me? Had she gotten excited and struggled she would have torn her legs up badly. And, had he not gone down the road at that particular time, she would probably have died from the heat.

We walked up to her very slowly and all the time I was talking very calmly to her so she would not struggle. Easy girl, that's a good girl, easy girl. All of a sudden a light came on in my brain reminding me of something I heard once at a seminar. Maybe I heard it even more than once. My memory reminded me, if you have a horse down and you put pressure on her head/neck she cannot get up. I said to the ranch hand, gently put your knee on her neck and keep her from trying to get up.

All the while I continue to talk calmly to the mare reassuring her that help was at hand.

Without putting myself in too much of an awkward position, as not to get hurt, I cut the wires with the bolt cutters one by one until all wire was off her hind legs.

When this was completed we let her get up. The mare was still very calm. Not once did she act upset. There were no lacerated areas on her legs, just had some imprinting where the wires had dug into her legs.

We walked her back to the ranch, did hydro therapy with cold water and gave her some oral bute. We then turned her out in a nearby pasture. We checked the mare the next morning and she was fine. She had no swelling or lameness.

Moral: Bits of information stored in the brain, came to surface when needed. Information that prevented this from a more serious outcome.

Another boring seminar, eh? It paid off.

AL NAKIB

Tying-Up Syndrome...

The term tying up in horses characterized by muscle stiffness and pain; sweating, trembling, reluctance to move and often discolored urine (brown). It's usually triggered by excessive exercise. Tying up occurs when the energy supply to perform physical activity is insufficient. The horse may be agitated and even paw the ground. Blood tests will show elevated levels of muscle enzymes.

The medical term for tying up is Rhabdomyolysis which means skeletal muscle (rhado) breakdown/damage (lysis).

Sooo on this particular day, while stall cleaners were making their rounds, one of the guys noticed Al Nakib was looking and acting strange. The ranch hand alerted me. From my experience of similar cases and symptoms past, I knew that we needed our veterinarian to examine and medicate the horse. The suspected diagnosis was confirmed. Dr. S administered bicarbonate of soda to Al Nakib and said to keep an eye on him.

Apparently we did not check on him as often as we should, so once again one of my workers came and told me that Al Nakib looked bloated. The medication given him for the tying-up made him very thirsty. Since he had an automatic waterer in his stall he drank as much water as he wanted to quench his thirst. Not good....

I called Dr. S again who gave him diuretics and said to hand walk him often so he would urinate and get rid of the excess fluids. Peculiar to the horse he would not, would not, would not urinate in the stall. You would have to take him onto grass before he would pee.

By " dark:thirty", I knew that this was going to be an all night session. We moved Al Nakib to the main barn where we had a double stall. I would walk back and forth from house to barn about every 30 to 40 minutes halter him and lead him out of the stall. The instant I walked him onto the grass, he stopped and peed. By 10:00 p.m. I needed to make a change to this back and forth to house routine. So I put the lounge chair in corner of stall. Got into some warmer clothes to withstand 40 degree temperature and settled in for the night.

Again, about every 30 to 40 minutes, Al Nakib and I would go out, and yes, every time we hit the grass he stopped, spread his legs and would urinate.

Towards early morning, I knew he was much better because he would come over to where I was sleeping and nuzzle my feet. As if to say hey, I'm better, thanks to you.

Gus was going duck hunting that morning, so he decided to stop and have a look at Al Nakib and Eskimo me. That's what he said when he saw me. "You look like and Eskimo." I told him earlier in the evening I really thought we would be loading this horse in the trailer for LSU veterinary clinic. He was that bad and I was concerned…. But since we had walked off and on all night he was doing great.

Oh, by the way, did I tell you that this? Al Nakib was a stallion. Oh not just any stallion, but an Egyptian Arabian Stallion. You know the ones people say are crazy and dangerous. Ha. Not a mean bone in his body. When I tell people this story about me sleeping in stall all night with one of my stallions, they think I am kidding.....Not kidding and yes I did.

Many years later Al Nakib was sold to a gentleman from Cairo.

We made the decision because Al Nakib had such special genes that were almost extinct and we were not breeding him at this time. So I reluctantly sent him to Egypt. There he could continue preserving his blood lines.

I was told that Al Nakib had settled many mares and produced beautiful foals.

Big Al, you are missed.

HEALTHY HORSE

The Importance of Deworming Program..

I always tell potential horse buyers/owners that whatever you pay for the horse, is the least amount you will spend on that horse. The overall caring for the horse falls under many categories.

In my estimation the most important item on horse care is a deworming program, a regular deworming program.

There are some areas we live in that I call, the parasite capital of the world. Southeast Texas is one them. The heat and humidity are perfect weather condition for parasites to survive.

When I was having "equine summer camps", for juniors and adults, I taught safety around horses and total care which included immunizations, deworming programs, grooming along with learning the anatomy. You can best understand your horse if you know what makes him "work".

Your immunization and deworming program depends on where you are located and what your veterinarian recommends. All horses that are in your care should be on the same schedule of deworming.

On our farm we use a paste dewormer every two months, rotating from one type to another. Then once a year, we have our veterinarian tube worm the horse. On this visit the horses teeth are checked and floated if needed.

Back to summer camp: many times while campers were bathing or grooming their horses, the horse would defecate. Uhhhhh was usually what we heard. I would tell them that was perfectly normal and oh so necessary. Instead of just cleaning it up, they needed to look at the manure to see if it was more or less normal.

Was it firm, was it like a "cow pie" or runny? Also did you see anything unusual in the manure?

Sometimes days after deworming, you would see dead strongyles or Bot fly larva. Once when I looked down at what a horse had just deposited, it was like a "cow pie" and there were thousands and thousands of small living strongyles.

This particular horse had not been on our ranch for very long and even though he supposedly was up to date on immunizations and deworming, he still had many, many parasites in him.

We checked with the veterinarian, who suggested we tube worm him, since the paste worming did not take care of the infestation.

At this part of the story let me tell you about all the damage parasites can to do the horse. Most people think worms are confined to the stomach or intestines. No.....

LUNG WORMS larvae are ingested and migrate to the vessels of the lungs.

LARGE STRONGYLES larvae mature in the intestinal tract. There are two types that migrate into the liver.

SMALL STRONGYLES burrow into the wall of the colon. Most damaging of internal parasites and are resistant to most dewormers.

(refer back to the horse that had been dewormed and still had many, many small strongyles.

ROUND WORMS Eggs develop into larvae which migrate to the liver, heart, and lungs.

TAPEWORMS attach to intestinal lining

PINWORMS lay eggs in the skin around the horse's anus.

STOMACH WORMS can cause mild diarrhea. Larvae can get in open sores on the horse's skin and cause "summer sores"

THREAD WORMS mostly a concern in foals. Mainly cause is diarrhea.

BOTS Adult bot flies (remind you of bees) will be hovering around the horse at times when you are grooming. The fly lays its eggs in areas where the horse can ingest them. Larvae hatch and burrow in the gums and tongue to develop more. Then on to the stomach and intestines before passing out in the manure. Large numbers of bots have been associated with gastric ulcers.

FILARIAL parasites. (neck threadworm) These parasites live in the ligament that runs along the horse's neck between withers and poll.

There are many, many other parasites, but the whole purpose is to show you that more than the intestines are affected by parasites. Therefore regular deworming is important, but still may not keep your horse free of these parasites. Record keeping is an important part of horse management.

The horse mentioned earlier in this section, died from what was determined to be an aneurysm probably due to parasite damage at an earlier age. The horse was four years old at the time of his death.

DABASK

Here Kitty, Kitty...

Living on a ranch you usually have a menagerie of animals. Some you added and many, many others that just showed up. LOL In our case many times, our great grandchildren living next door helped increase the numbers. "Oh Nanu, it is so cute. Look what showed up here at the ranch. Can we keep it?" You get the picture.

So it was this darling little grey cat that showed up and took charge. She wondered around getting acquainted with everyone. Even the horses. One in particular "DABASK". She would wonder around his stall and paddock, walk up and down the fence and DABASK would follow her and nuzzle up to her. Awwww they had become best buds.

This continued on and we all thought it was so cute. He was such a gentle horse anyway. Did I tell you he was a stallion, but not a mean bone in his body.

One weekend we had a family stop by to visit the ranch and see the horses. We were happy to give them the two bit tour. We showed them each and every horse. Of course a story goes with each one.

We made our way to the stallion stalls and paddocks and there was sweet DABASK. We were talking about him, how kind and gentle he was and he came over to fence for all to pet him.

In the meanwhile little grey cat showed up and as before hopped up on the top board of fence and was walking up toward DABASK. I told the visitors how the cat and DABASK had become great friends and how he nuzzled the cat. So cute I said.

Well......about that time DABASK grabbed the cat, threw her to the ground and tried to stomp her. Oh my, there were children in this group too. Thank goodness in trying to stomp her, he was unsuccessful in hurting her. I was shocked and so were they.

That friendship had just ended. I would imagine the little grey cat decided that her odd friendship was not a good idea anymore and went about being thankful she still had eight lives left.

ZAARAFIC

You Can't Make Me If I Don't Want to.....

We talk a lot about the mares, but let's not forget about the "Guys". Without them we wouldn't need the mares.....well then maybe we would.

Anyway I wanted to tell you a little bit about a gentleman stallion we owned who truly had a mind of his own. He was a kind, obedient and beautiful moving grey/white stallion named ZAARAFIC.

In the performance ring he really showed off his stuff. The more the crowd reacted to his performance classes,, the better his action was. He was a fancy English Pleasure and (back in the old days) a Park Horse. Things have since changed in that category of horse shows.

Now on a different note, if you wanted to do something to him or with him that he really did not want to do...guess who won. I don't normally go along with letting the horse win, but I learned early that it wasn't worth the fight. The easier route was taken.

For instance: When it came to tube worming this stallion there was no way it could be done. We had a young veterinarian at that time who made a call to tube worm all the horses here on the ranch. I explained to him that it was impossible to tube this particular stallion and that others had tried and failed. He would not accept my excuses and decided that he would indeed tube worm ZAARAFIC.

He tried and tried and fought and fought to get the tube down. He tried every trick that he knew to no avail. He finally gave up and paste wormed the horse. From then on paste worming was all we did on him..

Another example of his attitude…"you can't make me" ..I had left the ranch to run some errands and when I returned home the farrier was there working on ZAARAFIC..

It was a miserable hot day and the farrier and trainer had tried everything they knew to get the job done. The horse had been twitched, snubbed to the wash rack wall and tranquilized.

The farrier explained that he had three shoes already in place and every time he picked up the fourth hoof (left rear) the stallion tried to kick him. He had one nail in that shoe. They should have realized that they had pushed him just a little too far.

I was very upset with this situation and commented to the trainer that it was common knowledge to everyone at the ranch that you could not force this guy to do anything. Why had they pushed him so far? I told the farrier to stop and asked if he could show me the nails. He said the nails are designed and marked so that when nailed a certain way it would come out to the side. There is a design on one side of the nail to indicate how it should be positioned. I told him I had the tools I needed and I would attempt to nail the shoe later in the day when it was cooler and ZAARAFIC had settled down. Oh sure, the trainer thought.

Later that evening, just before dark, I told my husband I was going to the barn and if I didn't come back in about thirty minutes to come check on me. I should have known that remark was unnecessary.

My plan was to be very calm and subtle in what I had planned to do.

With tools in hand and horseshoe nails ready, I went into ZAARAFIC'S stall. He was calmly grazing in his paddock. I haltered him and loosely tied him in his stall. I gently picked up his left rear hoof, softly talking to him and awkwardly but gently I nailed the shoe in place. He never attempted to pull the hoof out of my hand or move away from me. He did not feel he was being forced or threatened. He allowed me to nail on the shoe because he wanted to be cooperative.

On another occasion, we were having a Christmas Party at the ranch when one of the guests who had gone out to the barn to see the horses came in the house very upset. While out in barn, they noticed that ZAARAFIC was down and acting colicky.

It just so happened that we had two of our veterinarians attending the party, my long time friend Dr. Sherwood and one of his associates.

We put ZAARAFIC in the stock in the vet room and Dr. S began examining him. They began inserting the stomach tube into ZAARAFIC'S nostril in order to put oil into his stomach and the stallion made no effort to fight us or give us any trouble while this happening. He knew we were all trying to help him and he was cooperative.

After oiling him and giving him pain medication, time passed and ZAARAFIC became worse instead of better. Dr. S suggested we take him to LSU Large Animal Clinic in Baton Rouge, Louisiana ASAP.

Shortly after arriving at LSU, ZAARAFIC was taken to surgery for an obstruction in the colon. He lived two days after surgery and died of complications.

He will be remembered fondly, as the stallion who did what you wanted him to do because he respected you and trusted you. Not because you tried to force him to do anything.

Beautiful ZAARAFIC

KEB

Oh Yes, I Know Each One Personally ...

I received a phone call one day from an attorney, a lady. Her conversation began with, "Mrs. McFaddin I am Mrs. Jones (not her real name) an attorney in this area and I am representing someone who owns a horse that was bought from you, but you probably won't remember the horse".

My reply was "mam I have been a breeder for fifteen years (at that time) and I know each and every horse on a very personal basis. I breed them, foal them out, and care for them when they are sick. I love them. How could I not know each and every one of them?

People have horses for different reasons. We have them because we love them and they are a very big part of our lives. Some more so than others. Here's an example of a special one that I personally knew.

KEB was one of those big, bold and beautiful animals that I put a lot more than the usual amount of love and care into.

I did his training from the ground work up, believe me I am not a trainer. He was so trusting and loving that training him was easy. Now mind you he had a big mouth and we were constantly working on that. He liked to talk. When he was out in his paddock and someone would pass by, he would whiny as if to say, "hey here I am". Also when you were working him under saddle, he felt it necessary to call out to his nearby friends.

His first show under saddle was our May Beaumont show and we were a long way from being a "finished pair". He was so willing, so beautiful and so much like his sire, El Ibn Fabah. He had so much potential. I looked forward to another athletic, beautiful, versatile Arabian like his sire. I looked forward to many years of riding and just being around this guy.

On the morning of July 21, after being in the paddock all night he was found to have an injured leg. The cause was undetermined.

KEB was taken to LSU veterinary hospital. The diagnosis was fractured left radius, prognosis—poor. KEB was euthanized July 22.

KEB was a three year old straight Egyptian stallion out of SERENITY YOSREIA and EL IBN FABAH.

We miss you KEB. We miss your beauty, your willingness and your loudness. We miss you as an individual.

For whatever reason Mrs. Jones had called, I am sure we had a good conversation and she was convinced that I indeed knew my horses.

Each and everyone of them.

KEB was just one example.

AMIR FASEER

Took a Piece of My Heart/My Prince

You will remember the story about Fanny, my first introduction to horses? Needless to say my love and desire to own horses has continued. Now I will tell you about my great love for AMIR FASEER, straight Egyptian stallion.

So Fannie was the first horse and after writing all the experiences that I have had as a horse owner, I must say something about the greatest horse that ever lived, as far as I am concerned.

Gus and I were in the early phase of our breeding program and we already had a couple of stallions. Gus had heard about and read about the Babson Arabian Farm. Henry Babson was a breeder of the Egyptian Arabian horse from around 1893 until his death in 1970. Babson horses were well known for their impeccable dispositions and their fantastic blood lines. Very interesting reading if and when you have time.

Anyway, we planned a trip to visit Babson Arabian Farm with the thought in mind to purchase a young colt, not just any colt, but one with particular blood lines to enhance our breeding program.

After meeting with Mr. Watson, the Babson manager for many, many years, we told him what our interest was and he directed us to the mares that had foals by their sides. "Now I'm not going to tell anything about pedigrees" he said, just let you see for yourself and decide what appeals to you". He turned and walked away leaving us in a pasture with the most beautiful mares and babies we had ever seen. It didn't take us too long to "hone in" on a beautiful very dark, almost black, little fella.

We walked a bit closer then just stood there, and he wondered over so we could get a better look. Now mind you his dam was a beautiful sight to see as well.

We did look over the entire herd, but we kept coming back to that little dark guy. (That little dark horse stayed dark for a very long time before turning grey). He was always beautiful.

When Mr. Watson came back, we pointed out the colt that we really liked and he said, "why sure" you have probably picked out the best colt in the group and for sure the best mare. He showed us the pedigree and Gus was impressed.

A price for the colt was discussed, which we thought was very reasonable. The purchase was complete and we were told that when the colt was weaned, he could be transported to us. We were very excited.

Before his arrival, we transferred his papers to our name and decided to name him AMIR FASEER since his sire was FASEER. Mother's name was AROUFINA. AMIR meaning Prince, and indeed he was true royalty.

After being weaned he was transported to us, and I knew right away, this was the special horse for me.

Jean and Amir Faseer

Now, you will remember that when our mares foaled, we were hands 'on' with the foal from day one. Well…I don't think that was the case with "AMIR" as he was lovingly called by all. He may have been halter broke but that was about all. Standing tied, baths without incident, cleaning feet, trimming feet oh no, it was a fight. We always won.

He gave the farrier so much trouble one time that the farrier said " if I had the money you paid for him, I would buy him and kill him". Well........I never. This was certainly not what a farrier or anyone else should say.

I have since learned in most instances that most foals are not handled the way we handle ours.

We put a halter on them, morning after they are born. We walk with them just a little with their mom. (no lead rope). When they are in our arms we rub them all over, up and down their legs. Did I mention when they are born we imprint them and it really shows off over time.

Over a period of time AMIR soon learned that he was a big boy and needed to go with the flow.

He grew into a beautiful young stallion, and when he was ready to be trained to saddle, I sent him to a wonderful young woman named Francie. She did wonders with him. He was trained and shown Western pleasure, Hunter Under Saddle, Mounted Native Costume and Trail.

He won many times in all these classes but he was a champion when it came to being a Trail Horse. He was the greatest one ever. Blue ribbons won at almost every Arabian horse show he entered. At Regionals he was champion. All this credit goes to Francie. She loved AMIR almost as much as I did. Francie taught AMIR to bow and many times when it came time to take his winning picture, he would not cooperate with ears forward and looking like a champion, so Francie would have him bow receiving his blue ribbon.

Frances Frobese Newsom

Another thing she taught him was to stretch. Legs forward, hind legs back somewhat. This brought his back down quite a bit and it was very helpful at times mounting him. Particularly me.

I began participating in classes at the same time Francie was showing him so she could instruct me as well as AMIR. AMIR and I did so, so, but I can tell you when I won that first blue ribbon in Western Pleasure I was so excited I think I trotted around the judges stand several times. I also cried when I left the ring. I don't think Francie was with me at that time, but I know she would have been proud.

Now I have talked about his training and his accomplishments but I have forgotten to tell you the most important characteristic of AMIR. He had an impeccable disposition. He never, ever tempted to bite or kick or act in anyway but a gentleman. He was so well mannered that I did not hesitate to let juniors ride him. In fact my great grandson, Jesse, showed him at one time. Juniors could lead him around, bath and groom him, and he was always "perfect".

We later added Side Saddle to his show career and that was really fun. Don't think I blew everyone away in this class, but I can tell you Amir and I looked good and we had a great time.

Let me say at this time that AMIR sired many beautiful foals. However he had a few breeding peculiarities or maybe personality quirks. A funny one was when it came time to lead him up to a mare that he was to breed he needed to be in the mood. We sometime said, jokingly, that we needed to play romantic music for him. He was funny also about color of the mare. If the mare was grey, he would sort of snort and maybe want to pull you over to where the grass was and graze instead of breed. Oh, Oh.

We finally decided that he liked dark mares sooooo, we would go and get a bay mare, (could have been a bay gelding) and just approach the area where the mare to be bred was tied. He would look up, see the bay, whinny and we then would direct him to the grey mare. Okkkkk mission accomplished. Turn off the music and take away the "bay horse".

I have so many wonderful memories of my times on AMIR. I loved riding up and down the big ditches near us, riding over in the hay fields.

One time some cows had gotten on our property and I decided AMIR and I would take off after them. With ears back and at a very fast gallop we pursued the cattle. His ears, not mine. I remember Kathy Marcum who worked with me at the time, being in that pasture and riding with me when AMIR as I took off. A Prince turned cow horse. He was indeed another versatile Arabian horse.

On other occasions while riding AMIR towards the hay fields, I would stop and pick up my two year old great granddaughter, Chelsee, who lived next door. She would sit in front of me in the saddle and away we would go. There is no way I would take a chance of a stallion acting up while I had a small child riding with me. No problem with AMIR. Needless to say that precious two year old loved every minute of that ride.

AMIR and I were the best of friends. I truly loved that horse. We shared many "happy trails" together. In fact when I would ride him out in the hay field or ditches, sometimes I would sing for a while "happy trails to you"…until we meet again.

I lost my friend and companion when he was 28 years old. Like always in the past I had to make the decision to do the right thing and not let him suffer. His health had deteriorated to the point that when he laid down, he sometimes could not get up.

My veterinarian came to the ranch and with understanding and compassion, he helped AMIR out of his suffering and on to the greener pastures. This had to be one of the most difficult times with my horses that I have ever had. I held his head and watched as he took his last breath. My heart stopped for a minute. This beautiful animal that had been so much a part of my life was no longer. Maybe he didn't go to greener pastures, but is racing across the desert with a band of beautiful bay mares.

Since AMIR was no longer with us, I lost the desire to put myself into another horse as I did with him. I love all my horses, but something inside me died when he died.

Anyone who is blessed to have an animal, or horse that you are mentally and physically in tune with can relate to the story that I have told you about AMIR.

There is always that very special one.

Tears in my eyes now.

Jude and Jean

ACKNOWLEDGMENT

Thank you for your input is such a simple, weak comment to a dear friend who has been by your side and in your life for many years.

Our friendship started with the horses many years ago but has evolved to being family big time. She is always there when I need her or for that matter when anyone needs her. She is the kindest, sweetest, most patient person you will ever meet. When I sent her the stories from this so called book, I knew I could count on her to set me straight. The ins, ands, and buts plus comments that she inserted into these episodes made the writings more understandable for readers. She has been a great part of many of these experiences that I talk about. The first time she was in attendance at a foaling was here at the ranch. She could write a short story on that event. I hope and pray that as long as I live she will be my ins, ands, and buts in whatever I pursue. Life with my friend by my side. Jude Laminack

Jean McFaddin 2010 with some of her babies

Printed in the United States
By Bookmasters